The Seventh Trumpet

The Seventh Trumpet
The Rapture Question Answered

Pastor Clay Kendall

Xulon Elite

Xulon Press Elite
2301 Lucien Way #415
Maitland, FL 32751
407.339.4217
www.xulonpress.com

© 2023 by Pastor Clay Kendall

All rights reserved solely by the author. The author guarantees all contents are original and do not infringe upon the legal rights of any other person or work. No part of this book may be reproduced in any form without the permission of the author. The views expressed in this book are not necessarily those of the publisher.

Due to the changing nature of the Internet, if there are any web addresses, links, or URLs included in this manuscript, these may have been altered and may no longer be accessible. The views and opinions shared in this book belong solely to the author and do not necessarily reflect those of the publisher. The publisher, therefore, disclaims responsibility for the views or opinions expressed within the work.

Unless otherwise indicated, Scripture quotations taken from the King James Version (KJV) – public domain.

Paperback ISBN-13: 978-1-66287-315-7
Ebook ISBN-13: 978-1-66287-316-4

Contents

Editing Comments..vii
To Be Read First 1
Proper Protocol...9
Part One – Promoting False Doctrine 17

Chapter One: I Thessalonians 4:13-18..........................19
Chapter Two: Matthew 24:37,38................................27
Chapter Three: Revelation 4:1 31
Chapter Four: Revelation 3:10,11 35
Chapter Five: The Missing Churches After Revelation three 41

Part Two – Hiding the Truth 47

Chapter One: II Thessalonians 2:1-12 49
Chapter Two: Grace Means Tribulation for Christians.............57
Chapter Three: Cloven Tongues.................................59
Chapter Four: The Rapture Theory..............................61

Editing Comments to Reader

Annotations to be observed:

1. With the highest respect for the Living God, I capitalize in the third person: He, Him, His, and Himself. This also includes capitalizing the Holy Spirit, the Word, Messiah, Living God, Savior.

2. I accept and use Apostle Paul as the Hebrew writer.

3. Throughout the book, all Hebrew and Greek definitions are taken from the latest edition of the James Strong's Concordance (also abbreviated the Strong's Conc.).

4. All Bible references and quotes are from the King James Version (KJV). Only occasionally did I modernize wording for clearer understanding.

To Be Read First

There are several lessons we can learn from studying the Bible, but perhaps none are more important than to understand the depth of Satan's wickedness, and his ability to deceive Christians using scripture. Truly, Satan knows the Bible better than most Christians, and he uses it to his advantage. Moses warns us about his cunningness early in the book of Genesis. He said that the serpent is the most subtle beast in the field (Gen. 3:1); this is to say that Satan is the most deceptive entity the world has ever known. Too many people are oblivious to this fact, and this is why they are easily deceived. In fact, many people deny his existence. And to those who know better, he is like a snake camouflaged in front of them, and they are caught off guard when he attacks them.

Yet, by watching any local or world news outlet, anyone can easily recognize that there is an evil presence at work in every corner of the world. To deny that there is a devil, or a Satanic influence behind all of the horror we see today, is like denying one's own birthright. Truly, the lack of Bible knowledge preserves Satan's anonymity.

This book is not designed to convince people that Satan does exist. This would be like writing a book to prove $1+1=2$, or to prove that humans need air to breath. Some things are too obvious and instinctively clear to require a book to explain them. However, what is needed in this world, especially in the Christian world, is a book to explain the depth of Satan's lies, his daily method of operation, and how to defeat him at his own game.

Jesus taught about these things. After He was tempted by the devil forty days in the wilderness, He gave three examples of how to defeat him. Quoting scripture was essential (note verses 4, 7, and 10 of Matthew chapter four):

Then was Jesus led up of the Spirit into the wilderness to be tempted of the devil. 2. And when he had fasted forty days and forty nights, he was afterward a hungered. 3. And when the tempter came to him, he said, if thou be the Son of God, command that these stones be made bread. 4. But he answered and said, it is written, Man shall not live by bread alone, but by every word that proceedeth out of the mouth of God. 5. Then the devil taketh him up into the holy city, and setteth him on a pinnacle of the temple, 6. And saith unto him, if thou be the Son of God, cast thyself down: for it is written, He shall give his angels charge concerning thee: and in their hands they shall bear thee up, lest at any time thou dash thy foot against a stone. 7. Jesus said unto him, it is written again, thou shalt not tempt the Lord thy God. 8. Again, the devil taketh him up into an exceeding high mountain, and showeth him all the kingdoms of the world, and the glory of them. 9. And saith unto him, all these things will I give thee, if thou wilt fall down and worship me. 10. Then saith Jesus unto him, get thee hence, Satan: for it is written, thou shalt worship the Lord thy God, and him only shalt thou serve. 11. Then the devil leaveth him, and, behold, angels came and ministered unto him. (Matt. 4:1-11)

Notice in verse six that Satan misquotes Psalms 91:11-12. It is only slightly altered, but it changes the meaning completely. Should we expect accuracy from the lips of the evil one? Twisting scripture to deceive the unlearned is one thing, but having the audacity to tempt Jesus with scripture is not only highly wicked, but beyond our imagination. Please notice the cunningness of Satan. He replaced four words (in all thy ways), with three words (at any time). Please observe the correct translation by King David:

> For he shall give his angels charge over thee, to keep thee in all thy ways. 12. They shall bear thee up in their hands, lest thou dash thy foot against a stone. (Ps. 91:11,12)

Satan implies that Jesus could sin, but the angels would be there to help Him overcome. However, on the contrary, David is emphatic to say that it is impossible for Jesus to sin, having the angels there to help Him. These are two contrasting statements about Jesus's divinity. Satan denies Jesus Christ's divinity as the Son of God; David declares Jesus Christ's divinity as the Son of God.

Much can be learned from this, but three things are noteworthy:

1. Christians must learn to use God's Word against Satan, not human logic. Man's reasoning will not fend off Satan. King Solomon said, "Trust in the Lord with all thine heart; and lean not unto thine own understanding. In all thy ways acknowledge him, and he shall direct thy paths," (Prov. 3:5-6).

2. Christians must understand what God's Word says and what it does not say. Paul said that Christians must study the Bible, and learn to rightly divide it (2 Tim. 2:15). It is worth adding that Satan works harder in the sanctuary than he does outside of it. Obstructing the validity of God's Word has been Satan's goal from the beginning. It breeds misinterpretations, and misinterpretations breed confusion. Satan's strategy is to divide God's people, and then conquer them.

3. Christians must not back down from Satan's attack against them. They must be bold, and use God's Word to defeat him. Luke wrote that every Christian has power over evil spirits, especially over Satan, through faith in Jesus Christ (Luke 10:18-19).

Learning to rightly divide God's Word is perhaps the most important of the three things mentioned. What good would it do to quote scripture if you did not understand the true meaning and significance of what you were quoting? Words are just words if you do not understand what they mean. Satan is no dummy; he is a scripture lawyer and highly intelligent. It is true that he is limited because he is not God, but he knows what God's Word says, and what it does not say. He knows what God's Word means and what it does not mean. He is supernatural and highly deceptive. Misunderstanding and misquoting scripture plays right into his hands. He is free to misquote scripture to deceive the unlearned, not the other way around.

It is a growing problem that many Christians complain about being confused about the Bible, and consequently, do not have the desire to read it on a daily basis. They feel frustrated when the secular world banters them with questions they cannot answer. They become frustrated, with no apparent recourse, when science establishes bona fide facts that supposedly oppose what was written in the Bible.

As a pastor, I have witnessed these things often, and in most cases, the problem lies in the fact that people misunderstand what the Bible truly teaches. Too many Christians profess things about the Bible that are not actually biblical. Sadly, they do not realize they are deceived. Spiritual complacency can cause some of these problems. Most Christians accept whatever their preacher says as the gospel truth, without researching the scriptures for themselves. This is unwise, and the Bible teaches against it.

So, why is there so much confusion about the Bible among so many Christians – those who should know better? There are several reasons, but I will narrow it down to three.

Most Christians are not taught how to study the Bible. It would seem that English speaking people think that the Bible was written in English; even as though the prophets of old spoke English. When they read the Bible, they translate the English meaning into their mind according Noah Webster's dictionary. This method can only lead to utter confusion. All Bible readers should know that the Bible was written in ancient Hebrew, Greek, and some Aramaic, not English.

Therefore, realizing that the King James Bible was not translated into English until 1611 A.D., it is by design that an English reader transliterate first, and then translate. This means that they must research the original Hebrew or Greek from English before translating the text. This is easily performed by using a Strong's or Young's Concordance. The Strong's is preferred among scholars and theologians.

A majority of Bible readers take for granted that the English translations today, of which there are countless, are equivalent in meaning to the original Hebrew and Greek manuscripts of two-thousand years ago. This is baffling, because an English word today is predominately not what a Hebrew or Greek word meant originally. There are other factors that determine proper interpretation, but the main point is to begin transliteration of the text before translating the text.

Another important fact to Bible interpretation is to understand the laws of language. This is a vast topic, but I will offer a short brief on the topic.

Bible readers must recognize that earthly analogies are used often throughout the Bible, and thus, are not to be taken literally, but figuratively. Analogies provide better insight as to what is actually being said and intended. Jesus taught in parables for the same reason. They come in many forms, such as idioms, metaphors, allegory, similitudes, etc., but all in all, they are figurative speech. Jesus taught this to Nicodemus when He said: If I have told you earthly things, and ye believe not, how shall ye believe, if I tell you of heavenly things? (John 3:12).

About this topic, the great E.W. Bullinger wrote:

> "A figure of speech is a designed and legitimate departure from the laws of language, in order to emphasis what is said. Hence, in such Figures we have the Holy Spirit's own marking, so to speak, of His own words. This particular form or unusual manner may not be true, or so true, to the literal meaning of the words, but it is more true to their real sense, and truer to truth," (E.W. Bullinger's Notes; Companion Bible, Appendix 6 – Kregel Publications Grand Rapids MI).

I say "Amen," to that. Too many Bible readers take what is meant to be figurative and take it literal; and what is meant to be literal they take figurative.

Christians must also be aware of the countless number of translations around the world; this is why there are so many denominations within Christianity. One church believes *this*, and another believes *that*, and still ten others believe something contrary to both of them. Only confusion can be the product thereof, and Satan is the mastermind behind it.

There are approximately 175,000 words in the English language (http://www.bbc.com/news/world-44569277.amp), and most words can mean, or be manipulated to mean, more than one thing. This is why the translators of the 1611 Original Edition of the English Bible (Thomas Nelson Publishers,

New York) wrote a very lengthy letter to the reader, warning them about the complexity of their work. In short, they strongly encouraged the reader to be aware of the many errors in it, i.e., errors in the English translation, not in the original Hebrew and Greek from which it was transliterated.

The KJ translators made these comments about their own work:

Page 1: "It is welcome with suspicion instead of love..." and "it is sure to be misconstrued, and in danger of being condemned."

Page 5: "No cause therefore why the word translated should be denied to be the word, or forbidden to be current, notwithstanding with some imperfections and blemishes may be noted in the setting forth of it."

Page 11: "... we ought to savor our work more of curiosity then wisdom."

In sum, to paraphrase a lengthy letter, they urge Bible readers to call upon the Holy Spirit for guidance, and not to literalize every word. They encourage the reader to meditate upon it day and night, and to study it, not only read it. They quote Saint Augustine to make their point clearer (page 7): "O, let thy scriptures be my pure delight, let me not be deceived in them, neither let me be deceived by them."

The main point of the translators is to acknowledge their deficiencies and limitations. Since the English language has countless words that have more than one meaning, it explains why the Bible must be first transliterated from the Old Testament and New Testament to attain proper interpretation. Fortunately, unlike the inconsistent English language, Hebrew and Greek are unique to tri-consonantal roots to lock-in and deepen thought and meaning.

Proper Protocol

To expound further on translating Scripture, it would be fitting to offer a few examples of how the English language has been misinterpreted throughout the Bible, and how a Christian should approach Bible interpretation. We will use the King James Version (KJV) in the examples given because it can be cross-referenced to the Strong's Concordance (hereafter, Strong's Conc.), which is a bridge to the original languages of Hebrew and Greek. This makes it much more useful to obtain accurate interpretations. No other translation can make this claim. All other versions are solely dependent upon the inconsistent nature of the English language, and only a few of them, in part, align with the original text.

Example one: In Luke 14:26, Jesus said to the multitudes that were following Him:

> If any man come to me, and hate not his father, and mother, and wife, and children, and brethren, and sisters, yea, and his own life also, he cannot be my disciple.

When we interpret this passage in English, we find that it contradicts the fifth commandment to "honor thy father and mother," (Exod. 20:12; Deut. 5:16). Yet, Jesus said that to be His disciple, we must hate our father and mother – even our wife, children, brethren, sister, and ourselves. Acknowledging the fact that Jesus would not contradict His Father's commandments, what did Jesus exactly say and mean?

Common sense tells us that we have an obvious mistranslation from Greek to English. But what is it? Did Jesus mean that believers are to hate the sinful actions of parents, family, friends, and even themselves, to be His disciples? If this was true, then why is it not written that way? Can we simply add words to the Bible to make it say what we want it to say? According to Revelation 22:19, God forbids adding or subtracting from His Word. So, what can we learn from this example?

The key word in this passage is "hate." It is the Greek *miseo,* which means "to love less." In other words, to be a disciple of Jesus Christ, a person must love their father, mother, brother, sister, even themselves, less than they love the Lord. They must put Jesus Christ first in their lives, and follow what He taught. They should not be influenced by any man or woman who would turn them away from the Gospel.

The word "hate" is an unfortunate translation. Of over sixty different English translations, only the Living Bible translates Luke 14:26 accurately. Yet, even if half of them were correct, how would a person know the original meaning without the use of a King James Bible and a Strong's Conc.?

Example two: In 2 Cor. 11:14, Apostle Paul states:

> No marvel; for Satan himself is transformed into an angel of light.

Now, with all due diligence to God's Word, we must ask ourselves, can Satan, the prince of darkness, actually translate himself into an angel of light? Can he actually change from evil to good? Can he be a righteous angel of light, and a wicked angel of darkness at the same time? All answers are in the negative.

So, what did Paul actually say and mean? The answer is found in the word "transformed." Using the Strong's Conc. as our guide, we learn that "transformed" corresponds to the Greek word *metaschematizo*, which means "to be disguised." Hence, Paul said that Satan can be disguised as, or have the appearance of, an angel of light, but he has no power to be anything righteous or good. He is the son of perdition because he has been judged to eternal damnation. At the end of the millennium, he will meet his eternal fate (Ezek. 28:18; Rev. 20:10). Sadly, many Christians interpret this passage as though Satan can amend his wicked ways at his own discretion. This is a great lie.

Example three: There are three passages in the book of Acts that present a major interpretation dilemma. The subject is Paul's conversion on the road to Damascus. In Acts 9:7, it states that the men with Paul "heard" a voice, but saw no man. But, in Acts 22:7, it says that the men saw a light, but they "heard not" the voice of him that spoke to Paul. Then, in Acts 26:14, it states that "only Paul heard" a voice speaking to him.

In English, all three passages strongly contradict each other. However, in the original Greek, everything is made clear. In the first passage (Acts 9:7), the key word is "voice" (Greek, *phone*), which means "sound." Thus, the men heard a sound, but they did not understand what was being said. This is confirmed in the second passage (Acts 22:9) that the men saw a light, but they "heard not" the voice of him that spoke to Paul. The key word is "heard" (Greek, *akouo*), which means "to perceive with understanding." Thus, as the passage stipulates, the men with Paul heard the sound, but did "not perceive" what was being said.

The last passage is key to connecting each verse. It states that only Paul "understood" (Greek, *akouo*) what the Lord spoke to him (quotation marks mine):

> And when we were all fallen to the earth, "I heard a voice" speaking unto me, and saying in the Hebrew tongue, Saul, Saul, why persecutest thou me? *it is* hard for thee to kick against the pricks. (Acts 26:14)

Now, the question is, how would a Bible reader understand these passages without the Strong's Conc. to guide them?

Example four: In Acts 12:4, we have the word "Easter" transliterated from the Greek word *pascha* (Passover), which is an unfortunate and gross error. There is no meaningful connection between "*pascha*" and "Easter;" in fact, they diametrically oppose each other – one is biblical, the other is pagan. No author of any book in the Bible used the pagan term Easter in their writings, and only once does it appear in the New Testament translation, which is a palpable mistake.

Bible scholars concur that "Passover" is the only word that can be translated from *pascha*. Of the twenty-seven times "*pascha*" is recorded in the New Testament, twenty-six times it is translated correctly. Only once is it translated as "Easter," and for no apparent reason. Yet, the majority of Christians continue to use the pagan term "Easter," instead of "Passover" when celebrating the Resurrection Day. This one example shows the power of the serpent as the most subtle beast of the field.

Now, to be clear, the difference between Passover and Easter is immense, both linguistically and spiritually. This must be understood and profoundly corrected. Any common research on the word Easter shows that it is associated with, and grounded upon, sexual orgies performed by the ancients, where newborns were sacrificed to Molech and other pagan gods. She was the goddess of sex, love, beauty, political power, and war. In Babylon, she was the goddess, Ishtar. She was also called Innana by the Sumerians, Diana by the Greeks, Venus by the Romans, and Isis by the Egyptians.

The development of how and why Easter worked its way into Christian dogma is too extensive to share here; however, the serpent is at the forefront of this deception. I encourage all serious Bible students to research the facts of the history of Easter for themselves, so they will not be deceived.

Paul wrote that Jesus Christ became our "Passover," and believers are to keep the feast with purity and truth (quotation marks mine):

> Purge out therefore the old leaven, that ye may be a new lump, as ye are unleavened. For even "Christ our Passover": is sacrificed for us: 8. Therefore let us keep the feast, not with old leaven, neither with the leaven of malice and wickedness; but with the unleavened bread of sincerity and truth (I Cor. 5:7-8).

"To keep the feast with purity and truth," means to reject any paganistic rituals, wording, or practices that may find their way into Christian dogma (like the word "Easter" infiltrated the Church). Simply put, Easter represents the moral decadence of the pagan nations that stood against the righteousness of the God of Israel. Christians must realize that to celebrate Passover in the name of "Easter" is a great insult to God. This practice should be rejected and eliminated from all worshipping Christians.

Example five: In Romans 8:20-21, it says:

> For the creature was made subject to vanity, not willingly, but by reason of him who hath subjected the same in hope. [21] Because the creature itself also shall be delivered from the bondage of corruption into the glorious liberty of the children of God.

The key word here is "creature," (Greek, *ktsis*) twice recorded (verses 20-21). It is also mistranslated in verse 39 as "creature," however, the word creature is not the correct translation. *Ktsis* means "creation" or "nature." It has no connection to the word "creature." It is translated correctly in verse 22:

> For we know that the whole creation groaneth and travaileth in pain together until now.

Paul taught that God's creation, such as trees, grasses, vines of the earth, stones, hills, valleys, seas, rivers, oceans, etc., groan to return to perfect order, as it was in the first earth age. Scholars call this era "prehistory." It is a by-gone age where Satan first rebelled against God. Because of this, we now live in a second earth age of bondage and corruption; however, one glorious day, nature will return to perfection as it once was.

Example six: In the Old Testament, we have another mistranslation from Hebrew to English. Isaiah 45:7 reads, (God speaking):

> I form light, and create darkness: I make peace, and create evil: I the LORD do all these things.

Here, in English, it clearly says that God creates evil. Yet, what does it say in Hebrew? If God creates evil, then why is the world judged so harshly?

Again, let us use the Strong's Conc. to clear up any confusion. In the passage above, two words are key: "create" and "evil." Starting with "create" (Hebrew, *bara*), it means "to bring about," or "to allow." It is a word of wide meaning, so its sense has to be determined by context. Connecting this with "evil," which is the Hebrew *ra'ra*, the context is set in opposition to the word "peace." The opposite of peace is disturbance, calamity, or distress, which correlates to the meaning of *ra'a*. Hence, Isaiah wrote that God allows calamity in this world as a tool of correction to bring His children to repentance (Jer. 18:11; Amos 3:6, 5:13).

Example seven: Continuing in the Old Testament, let us observe Job 19:26 (Job speaking):

> And though after my skin worms destroy this body, yet in my flesh shall I see God.

Now, in English it is quite clear that Job says that he will see God in his flesh. However, this directly contradicts Paul's words in 1 Cor. 15:50:

> Now this I say, brethren, that flesh and blood cannot inherit the kingdom of God; neither doth corruption inherit incorruption.

So, if flesh and blood cannot inherit the kingdom of God as Paul so aptly states, which is to say, man cannot see God while in a flesh body, how can we rectify Job's words that he will see God in his flesh?

For starters, Paul is correct that no man can see God in the flesh. The key word is "flesh," which is the Hebrew word *bawar*. One of its prime meanings is "freshness," or "to be renewed." Connecting this with the first part of Job's statement that after his skin, worms destroy this body (flesh body), to Paul's words, that the saints will inherit a new incorruptible body in Heaven, we can easily deduce what Job was saying. After he died, he would see God in his fresh or renewed (incorruptible) body in Heaven.

Now, what can we learn from these seven examples set before us? The principal rule is not to depend on arbitrary interpretations of any translation in English without the use of the Strong's Conc. to establish proper interpretation. Great scholars lead by the Holy Spirit through centuries of arduous work provided as the tools required to study the Bible in its original language. This is promised by our Savior, that all men have access to the true Word of God. Let us not under-appreciate their glorious and honorable work. Much gratitude and honor are owed to each of them.

In conclusion, converting Hebrew or Greek into proper English is the foundation and design of the rest of this book. We will examine the most popular scriptures that promote an early rapture of the Church, including others that are deceptive and misleading. The ultimate goal is to show that the rapture theory was developed by a collection of false traditions and false translations into English. Sadly, because of this, many Christians believe that Jesus Christ will gather the Church before the Antichrist's reign in the tribulation. This lie will cause many of them to be unprepared mentally, physically, and spiritually for the tribulation days that will soon beset the world.

Yet, if the truth is told, the Bible reveals the truth to whosoever will listen. It says that the beast (Antichrist) comes with horns as a lamb, but speaks like a dragon. Or the same, that Satan will come with power and glory, looking like the Messiah, but he will speak with a fire of lies like a dragon (Rev. 13:11). Prophesy is all about timing; this is why Jesus often told His disciples to watch. This book is designed to shine light for those who are asleep, so they will have an opportunity to understand God's Word as it is written.

Part One

Promoting False Doctrine

CHAPTER ONE:
1 THESSALONIANS 4:13-18

But I would not have you to be ignorant, brethren, concerning them which are asleep, that ye sorrow not, even as others which have no hope. [14] For if we believe that Jesus died and rose again, even so them also which sleep in Jesus will God bring with him. [15] For this we say unto you by the word of the Lord, that we which are alive *and* remain unto the coming of the Lord shall not prevent them which are asleep. [16] For the Lord himself shall descend from heaven with a shout, with the voice of the archangel, and with the trump of God: and the dead in Christ shall rise first: [17] Then we which are alive *and* remain shall be caught up together with them in the clouds, to meet the Lord in the air: and so shall we ever be with the Lord. [18] Wherefore comfort one another with these words.

Verses 13-16 are perhaps the most misinterpreted scripture that have advanced the popularity of the early rapture of the Church. Much of the confusion is a product of circumventing the original Greek into English. As a result, Paul's message was distorted and a false gospel was conceived.

It should be noted that Paul was a learned scholar of the Old Testament, being raised under the tutelage of the renowned Gamaliel (Acts 5:34).

Naturally, he quoted the Old Testament, which was then called the Hebrew Scriptures or Tanakh, to teach Christians the "good news" gospel in the New Testament. Although he was not a Greek scholar, he communicated well to the locals by writing colloquial Greek – also known as "street Greek." Doubtless, he took notes from King Solomon who wrote about life after death (brackets my words):

Or ever the silver cord be loosed, or the golden bowl be broken, or the pitcher be broken at the fountain, or the wheel broken at the cistern [after death]. ⁷ Then shall the dust return to the earth as it was: and the spirit shall return unto God who gave it (Eccl. 12:7).

Here, the wisest of all kings clearly taught that after death all souls, good and evil, returned to God who gave them life; the apostle believed the same thing. Paul wrote that, in the twinkling of an eye at the seventh trumpet, all flesh would be changed into new incorruptible bodies (1 Cor. 15:50-52). Both Solomon's discourse about life after death, and Paul's discourse about life after death, are one and the same doctrine.

Holding to this premise then, and with the understanding that proper interpretation is a by-product of holding to the subject and context of a given scripture in its original language, and not to deviate from it, Paul's discourse to the Thessalonians is made perfectly clear. First, he wanted them to know what happens to a soul after death. This includes both believers and nonbelievers, even those who also which sleep in Jesus (physical death), and even others who have no hope.

Secondly, his purpose was to comfort those who mourn. He assures them that those who sleep in Jesus will return with Him at the last trumpet (seventh). Noting that this was not possible if they were bound to the grave, he wanted them to know that they could celebrate the fact that their fellow brothers and sisters who died in Christ are in heaven, waiting to return with Him one glorious day.

> For if we believe that Jesus died and rose again, even so them also which sleep in Jesus will God bring with him.[14]
> ... we which are alive and remain unto the coming of the Lord shall not prevent them which are asleep.[15]

In verse 15, the key word is "prevent," (Greek, *phthano*), which means "to proceed." By definition and meaning, it confirms that the dead proceed to God (return to God) from which they came; moreover, we who are alive and remain cannot stop the process, nor would we want to.

Hence, Paul rightly explains where a soul goes after death. Pointing to Christians who die in Jesus Christ (accept Him), he says that they will return with Christ at the seventh trumpet. He adds that Christians who remain cannot prevent them, or proceed them, into heaven. This is what "the dead in Christ rise first" means: they go to heaven to be with the Lord before other Christians do. Fittingly, the translators place a colon (instead of a comma) after the words "the trump of God:" to show a pause in the text to punctuate the fact that "the Lord's return," and "the rising of the dead," are two separate events that occur at two different times.

It is worth repeating that "the dead in Christ shall rise first" means that Christians who die ascend to Heaven to be with the Lord before He returns to gather the Church. It does not mean, as it is often taught, that a collection of dead bodies will suddenly rise into the sky to meet the Lord in the air before the Church is gathered. For, if this was true, it would make void the solemn words of King Solomon, Ezekiel, Luke, John, and Paul.

Furthermore, how can Christians return with Jesus Christ from heaven if they are not already with Him? This alone destroys the notion that a decomposed body will rejoin a resurrected body in the air to complete the spiritual process of returning to heaven. This belief is irrational, and deserves no recourse. It is true that we all "groan within ourselves, waiting for the adoption, to wit, the redemption of our body," (Rom. 8:23), but the point Paul is making is quite apparent. All people want to purge their flesh body and put on incorruption. But it is unwise to think that God will reunite a perfect spiritual body in heaven with a centuries-old weathered body on earth to complete the process of perfection. Doubtless, once a person inherits an incorruptible body in heaven, it requires no help from a corpse on earth to make it more whole.

As mentioned, King Solomon taught this doctrine. He said that once a flesh body expires, it has "no more portion forever in anything under the sun," (Eccl. 9:6). In other words, a corpse has no mortal purpose in heaven or earth once the spirit is gone. This is because death initiates the redemption of a person's soul and spirit, which goes directly to the Father who gave it.

As it is written, Christian's must wait until the Lord's second coming to experience total bodily redemption. At this time, they are instantly taken to heaven in an incorruptible body, while the flesh is left to deteriorate in the earth from which it came. Having two bodies in one is called dualism. One body is corruptible and the other is incorruptible (1 Cor. 15).

Paul adds an important fact about this transformation. He wrote that the Lord will return by descending from heaven, which is initiated "by a shout, a voice of the archangel, and the trump of God." This is the last or seventh trumpet, as confirmed by Paul in his letter to the Corinthians (15:52).

Adding to this, according to Luke, there is a gulf fixed in Heaven, where Christians and non-Christians are separated from one another (Luke 16:26). Hence, all souls inherit an incorruptible body after death. This is why Luke said that, "God is not the God of the dead, but of the living: for 'all' live unto Him," (Luke 20:38). This means that all souls live under God's ultimate direction until the Great White Throne judgment, which comes after the millennium. Ezekiel agrees with Luke. He wrote that God owns all souls, and because of His great love, all men are judged fairly and justly (Ezek. 18:4-9).

The Bible teaches that there are two deaths for the wicked, and one for the saints. The wicked experience death of the flesh (first death), and the death of the soul, which comes after the millennium (second death). The saints experience only the first death, after which time, they inherit eternal life.

It goes without serious comment, that the fact that the word "revelation" means to reveal, not to hide, and it would be revealed to the saints in one of the trumpets, as recorded in Revelation 8:6-11:19, if a rapture of billions of Christians took place before the tribulation. John describes what happens in each trumpet to educate the saints about future events; and especially, when they gather back to Jesus Christ. It would be fitting then to analyze each of them, to see in which trumpet Jesus Christ returns to gather the saints:

Trumpet one: curses upon the earth. Trumpet two: curses upon the sea. Trumpet three: curses upon the rivers and fountains of water, and the spirit of bitterness (wormwood) inundates the world. Trumpet four: the sun, moon, and stars are smitten. Trumpet five (first woe): a locust army of wicked agents, who take on many forms, arrive on the world scene, to deceive the unlearned. Trumpet six (second woe): the fallen angels (like horsemen) return to earth, with Satan, the Antichrist (Rev. 12:9). This will be the pinnacle of wickedness around the world (Rev. 13:4). Trumpet seven (third woe): Jesus Christ returns in His Glory to gather the saints, and defeats the enemy at the battle of Armageddon (Rev. 11:15).

John makes it clear that Jesus Christ gathers the Church at the seventh trumpet, which comes after the tribulation. It is a grave mistake indeed to assume that the Church is taken before the seventh trumpet. This would place the rapture as early as the fifth or sixth trumpet, which is erroneous and unbiblical.

There is yet more to be exposed in Paul's writings about the false rapture doctrine. The word "and" (*and* the dead in Christ shall rise first), is *kai* in Greek, which is translated an astounding one-hundred different ways in the New Testament, meaning that, there is not one word that defines *kai*. Some of these include: *so, therefore; so, therefore; henceforth; hence; but; again; likewise; etc.* Undoubtedly, any of the nine words listed, and many more could be added, would have simplified the text. The King James translators could have easily translated Paul's words to say:

"... with the trumpet of God: *so*, the dead ..."
"... with the trumpet of God: *therefore*, the dead ..."
"... with the trumpet of God: *henceforth*, the dead ..."
"... with the trumpet of God: *hence*, the dead ..."
"... with the trumpet of God: *but*, the dead ..."
"... with the trumpet of God: *again*, the dead ..."
"... with the trumpet of God: *likewise*, the dead ..."

Even further, Paul was saying:

"... so, *my point about death is that* the dead ..."
"... therefore, *as I have so aptly stated*, the dead ..."
"... henceforth, *as pertaining to our topic*, the dead ..."
"... but, *as I have taught you*, the dead ..."

After laying forth these simple facts, let us now rightly understand verses 17 and 18 of Chapter 4.

When speaking of those who have not died unto the coming of the Lord, it is interesting that Paul wisely and purposely writes, "we which are alive and remain," to enlighten the fact that the dead have no function or future purpose remaining on earth. This means that they are not remaining in the ground, waiting for the redemption of their body, for the spirit and soul of the dead have already risen to be with the Lord. This act is the true definition of dust to dust and ashes to ashes (Eccl. 3:20; 12:7).

The words "and remain," are Paul's direct submission that only the living "remain." The dead do not remain in the ground for any reasonable purpose, for God is not the God of the dead, but of the living (Luke 20:38).

Now, to be "caught up," (Greek, *harpazo*) means simply to be gathered unto Jesus Christ in His "Spirit," (Greek, *aer*), at which time, the flesh will be transformed from a corruptible body to an incorruptible body. This happens only at the seventh trumpet.

It is true that the word "air" lends itself to think of the "sky." However, the Bible was not written in English so we must refer to the Greek to understand its correct meaning. It is the Greek word *aer* (spirit), which has nothing to do with clouds, sky, or the atmosphere. It refers to the Lord's Spirit, the breath of Life. The Greek word for "sky" is *ouranos,* which is not in the manuscripts. Therefore, when Jesus Christ returns with those who have died, the living will join them "together in one spirit," with the Lord.

Paul used "clouds" as a figure to form the concept of "a cloud of witnesses," having holy union with God, just as he used it in Hebrews 12:1 (quotation marks mine):

Wherefore seeing we also are compassed about with so great a "cloud of witnesses," let us lay aside every weight, and the sin which doth so easily beset *us* and let us run with patience the race that is set before us. (Heb. 12:1)

This is why Jesus Christ was called "the *cloudy* one." Numerous references in the Old Testament refer to the clouds in the same way (Ps. 97:2, 104:3; Dan. 7:13; Joel 2:2).

Returning to verse 17, note that the word "the" (in *the* clouds) is not in the original manuscripts; thus, as the great E.W. Bullinger points out in his side-column notes in the Companion Bible (1 Thess. 4:17), "the" is omitted, and the text should read "in clouds." That is to say, "in groups," likened to a cloud of birds, insects, or people. Thus, "in the clouds," does not correctly translate "in the sky," or "in the clouds of the air." This is very simplistic, clear, and a biblical doctrine relishing with common sense.

Chapter Two: Matthew 24:37-38

But as the days of Noe *were*, so shall also the coming of the Son of man be. ³⁸ For as in the days that were before the flood they were eating and drinking, marrying and giving in marriage, until the day that Noe entered into the ark ³⁹ And knew not until the flood came, and took them all away; so shall also the coming of the Son of man be. ⁴⁰ Then shall two be in the field; the one shall be taken, and the other left. ⁴¹ Two *women shall be* grinding at the mill; the one shall be taken, and the other left.

Here, we have an example put forth by Jesus, that is a replica of what will happen in the future before He returns at the seventh trumpet. He says that it will be like in the days of Noah. Most of us have heard the story of the great flood since childhood, so to keep our discussion simple and to the point, we will forego the deeper knowledge that the fallen angels will return to earth, like in the days of Noah. Let us examine instead the basic tenet that Jesus taught the disciples.

He said that during Noah's time men were "eating and drinking, marrying and giving in marriage until the day that Noah entered into the ark." This means that it was a wicked and unrestrained generation. Only a remnant was God-fearing; the rest were profoundly immoral. This involved sexual deviance and terrible iniquity against the daughters of Adam.

With this said, let us review verse 39 to see what Jesus said about the wicked: "And [they] knew not until the flood came, and took them all away; so shall also the coming of the Son of man be."

The first thing Jesus mentioned is that the wicked "knew not." This means that unbelievers will ignore the warning signs of prophecy put forth by Jesus. Only wise Christians will stay awake, be informed, and watch the fulfillment of Bible prophecy.

Jesus continues to say that, "the wicked were taken away by a flood." This act of being taken away happens from a flood no doubt, but it is not a flood of water, for God promised Noah that He would not flood the earth again. So, naturally, it will be an end-time flood of lies that will be cast out from Satan's lips, that will deceive the world, just as John reported (parenthesis and quotation marks mine):

And the serpent (Satan) cast out of his mouth water "as a flood" after the woman, that he might cause her to be carried away of the flood (Rev. 12:15).

Knowing that it is a spiritual flood of lies that Jesus was referring to (not physical water), we understand what Jesus was teaching. The "two in the field where one shall be taken, and the other left," means that one shall be taken away by Satan's flood of lies (deception), and the other will be left in the field working as Christ instructed, waiting for His return.

In other words, God will protect the wise from the Antichrist's flood of lies during the tribulation (quotation marks mine):

Chapter Two: Matthew 24:37-38

And the "earth helped the woman," and the earth opened her mouth, and swallowed up the flood which the dragon cast out of his mouth (Rev. 12:16).

The words, "and the earth helped the woman" are to be sharply noted. The woman represents the saints. We read that they will be helped on earth to fulfill their destiny to the seventh trumpet when Jesus Christ returns to gather them.

It is often heard that believers want to be the first ones taken. Yet, to their chagrin, they do not realize what they are indeed saying, for who would want to be taken away by Satan's lies? This is the mighty danger of the rapture theory. It teaches that the first one taken is going to heaven, when in fact, they will be taken in by the Antichrist's lies.

Jesus goes on to say that, "two women shall be grinding at the mill; the one shall be taken, and the other left." A mill is a grinding house where women churned flour to make bread. Jesus Christ is the "Bread of Life," so the implication is quite clear. Some Christians will take part of the great apostasy, and others will stay in the field working for the Lord.

This parallels Jesus's words about the five foolish virgins and the five wise virgins (Matt. 25:1-13). Make no mistake, a virgin is a woman that has not been seduced, so spiritually speaking, it means a Christian. Some Christians are wise and some are foolish. Hence, foolish Christians are taken in by the Antichrist's flood of lies, but the wise stay in the field spreading the gospel (grinding bread).

Jesus said, in Revelation 16:15: "Blessed is he that watcheth, and keepeth his garments [on]." The first ones taken no longer watch for Jesus, because they think they are present with Him. Not following the direction to "keepeth his garments on," means "taking your garments off" (to be wed to your husband).

This is why Jesus said, in Matthew 24:19, "Woe unto those that are with child in those days, and to them that give suck in those days." These are foolish Christians that become impregnated by the wrong husband (the Antichrist), and nurse his system of government. This will be a sad experience on the Lord's Day, especially for those who take interest in the things of the church, and are genuinely concerned about the souls of men. Sadly, listening to the traditions of men rather than God's Word is crucial in the last generation.

Chapter Three: Revelation 4:1

> After this I looked, and, behold, a door *was* opened in heaven: and the first voice which I heard *was* as it were of a trumpet talking with me; which said, Come up hither, and I will show thee things which must be hereafter.

This passage, for dubious reasons, is used to promote the rapture theory. Yet, there is much doubt among authoritative Bible teachers as to the legitimacy of such a claim. With a careful review into this matter, using sound biblical facts and clear documentation, it will soon become evident that a rapture of the Church has no place or connection in this passage.

Incredibly, rapture teachers claim that the first two words "After this," means "after the rapture," which places the incredible event between chapters 3 and 4. The alarming trouble with this premise is that there is no record, then, of the great event to be found in Scripture, since there is not a chapter or any obscure writing to be found between chapters 3 and 4 in Revelation. This is the problem of a "secret" rapture. It is so secret, in fact, that the apostle did not mention it.

What the apostle does mention in chapters 2 and 3, is Jesus Christ's address to the seven churches. Then, after this he reveals another vision in chapter four. This is clear and simple grammar. Only by deviating from the truth can a rapture of billions of people be inserted into John's writing.

As it is with the rules of language, once a subject and object are established, the basic meanings of words, context, etc., aid in determining proper meaning to the text. This prevents misleading concepts and convenient interpretations. Bible instructors should be restrained from interjecting a specific meaning to a text, without the proper laws of language to support their views.

It is worth mentioning that the last word in verse one, "hereafter," is transliterated from the same Greek word as "After this." It is the Greek word *meta tauta,* and it means "after these *things,*" which is plural. This proves that the interpretation after the rapture, which is a singular event, cannot stand. Simple research shows that *tauta* is never used in the singular (as in a singular event), but is used exclusively in the plural form. Most often, it is translated as "these things," which is far different than the singular tense, "after this."

Simply put, John wrote that a door opened in Heaven to allow him to come up hither so he could perceive a heavenly vision. Then, he was instructed to record what he saw in a book, which is the book of Revelation. Paul had a similar experience when he, and he *alone,* was caught up to the third Heaven to receive revelations from God (2 Cor. 12:2-7).

To clear up any misconceptions about our topic, let us review Revelation 4:2-3:

> And immediately I was in the spirit; and, behold, a throne was set in heaven, and *one* sat on the throne. [3] And he that sat was to look upon like a jasper and a sardine stone: and *there was* a rainbow round about the throne, in sight like unto an emerald.

Here, "I was in the spirit," means exactly what it says. John himself ("I") was in the spirit. He did not represent a group of individuals who were in the spirit. Full documentation is found in the fact that the Greek article is missing, showing that there is no emphasis pointing to the Church or any other group of people. Simply put, while John was in the spirit, God revealed another vision. He saw God sitting on the throne.

Further proof that John represented himself and not the Church is shown in the ascension of the two witnesses in Revelation 11:11-12 (quotation marks mine):

> And after three days and an half the Spirit of life from God entered into them, and they stood upon their feet; and great fear fell upon them which saw them. [12] And they heard a great voice from heaven saying unto them, "Come up hither." And they ascended up to heaven in a cloud; and their enemies beheld them.

The key words are "Come up hither" (Greek, *anabaino hode*). The Greek means the same as in English, "come up here," which is the same wording in 4:1. This continues a biblical precedence that men translated into heaven represented only themselves. Nowhere in the Bible has a man been taken to heaven, in the spirit or translated, that represented a group of people. This includes: the two witnesses, John, Paul, Moses, Elijah, or Enoch. We must neglect any temptation to interject our own preconceived ideas to define scripture without sound biblical exegesis to support it.

Chapter Four: Revelation 3:10-11

> Thou hast kept the word of my patience, I also will keep thee from the hour of temptation, which shall come upon all the world, to try them that dwell upon the earth.

Here again, we have rapture interpreters taking the liberty to define a meaning without using sound biblical principles.

To put this passage into context, Jesus Christ is praising the church of Philadelphia for having the knowledge of those "which say they are Jews, and are not, but do lie." In other words, they are aware of the globalists, who identify themselves as Jews, who control the world through the four hidden dynasties of education, economy, politics, and religion.

When Jesus said, "because thou hast kept the word of my patience, I also will keep thee from the hour of temptation," He was emphasizing that patience is a virtue. Christians are commended for having patience for it brings forth good works:

> And not only *so*, but we glory in tribulations also: knowing that tribulation worketh patience; ⁴ And patience, experience; and experience, hope: ⁵ And hope maketh not ashamed;

because the love of God is shed abroad in our hearts by the Holy Ghost which is given unto us (Rom. 5:3-5).

When speaking about the tribulation, Luke said, "in your patience, possess ye your souls," (Luke 21:19). In addition, John wrote that to follow Jesus Christ demands patience; and specially to overcome the mark of the beast (quotation marks mine):

He that leadeth into captivity shall go into captivity: he that killeth with the sword must be killed with the sword. "Here is the patience" and the faith of the saints (Rev. 13:10).

To fulfill God's plan, the saints need patience. Irrational emotions can only lead downward, as it unsettles the spirit and causes confusion. This is why the churches of Philadelphia and Smyrna were praised. They possess sufficient knowledge of Bible prophecy. They know that the end product of strong knowledge and faith in God is eternal salvation. This gives them a great sense of peace and stability when they see all the confusion around the world. They remain calm and firm in their beliefs, because Jesus said, "I have foretold you all things," (Mark 13:23). Hence, they are aware of the evil around them, and that Bible prophecy must come to pass as it is written.

This is not to say that a firm believer in the things God is pleased to see the world crumble into evil shards. It is more the fact that they understand that the problems in the world are a product of disobeying the Living God. Jesus said, "Ye shall know the truth, and the truth shall make you free," (John. 8:32). So, Christians are free in knowing that God is still on the throne, and that He is the judge of all things.

To take this one step further, when speaking about the tribulation, Jesus said:

> When they shall lead you, and deliver you up, take no thought beforehand what ye shall speak, neither do ye premeditate: but whatsoever shall be given you in that hour, that speak ye: for it is not ye that speak, but the Holy Spirit (Mark 13:11).

Not to premeditate is a direct commandment from Jesus Christ. Having patience will help the saints to wait on the Lord. Moreover, because of their patience, they are kept from the hour of temptation. When a person knows their destiny, and understands prophesy as it is written, there is no temptation to follow the Antichrist's scheme to control the world. In fact, He will be an abomination to the saints:

> For when they speak great swelling words of vanity, they allure through the lusts of the flesh, through much wantonness, those that were clean escaped from them who live in error (2 Pet. 2:18).

Peter's words are clearly stated: those who were clean, "escaped" from those who live in error. To escape means "to be free from temptation." The saints are set free from the confusion of this world while they are in the world. When praying to the Father about the saints, Jesus said (quotation marks mine):

> I pray, "not that thou shouldest take them out of the world, but that thou shouldest keep them from the evil," [16] They are not of the world, even as I am not of the world (John 17:15,16).

It is worth reviewing one last passage to sum up our discussion:

> And the dragon was wroth with the woman, and went to make war with the remnant of her seed, which keep the commandments of God, and have the testimony of Jesus Christ (Rev. 12:17).

The "remnant of her seed," is God's elect. It should be remembered that God uses little to accomplish much. Ezekiel especially makes this point known by emphasizing more than a few times, that although Israel would go astray and worship other gods, a remnant would be retained to fulfill God's will. This remnant has angered Satan throughout history, and in the end, he makes war with her again; however, this is a spiritual war, not a physical war. Satan wants her soul, not her flesh. Satan is fighting a losing battle, however, for she is protected by the Living God.

This war is called the hour of temptation, from which the Lord says, the remnant will be protected. This is because Satan is not a temptation to them. Instead, they see him as an abomination, and this is their escape. It is God's promise to the saints that they can escape the temptations and difficulties of Satan (quotation marks mine):

> There hath no temptation taken you but such as is common to man: but God *is* faithful, who will not suffer you to be tempted above that ye are able; but will with the temptation also "make a way to escape, that ye may be able to bear it." (1 Cor. 13:10).

The words "that ye may be able to bear it," show proof-positive that the saints must bear patience while going through temptations.

See references where "escape" is used in a spiritual sense: (Ps. 55:6-8; 71:2,18; 124:7-8; 141:10; Luke 21:36; 2 Pet. 1:4; 2:20).

Chapter Five:
The Missing Churches After Revelation 3

It has been alleged that the word "church," (Greek, *ekklesia*,) is not found after Revelation 3, thus proving that the Church has been "caught up," or "raptured" before the tribulation. However, before we would accept a lark as fact, let us review the following information.

1. The word *ekklesia* is found after Revelation 3. In fact, it is referenced to include all the churches in the last chapter. This shows that the Church encapsulates John's Revelation, front and back.

2. The stronger fact is that the word "Jews," (Greek, *Ioudaios*,) is not found after Revelation 3. Furthermore, the word "Jew" (singular) is not recorded in the entire book! Using rapture logic, are the Jews raptured with the Church? According to the rapture doctrine, the Jews' mighty purpose is to go through the tribulation, but where are they?

3. The word "Gentile" is not recorded in the entire book of John's Revelation. Does this mean not a single Gentile will be present in the tribulation? Amazingly, the plural "Gentiles" is recorded only once (Rev. 11:2).

4. The word "Israel" is found only twice after Revelation 3, and shockingly, only three times in John's entire Revelation. The plural form, "Jews," is recorded only twice. Yet, they are the prime participants in the tribulation.

5. Presented is a list of words that are not recorded after Revelation 3: Antichrist, sin, sinners, demons, wicked, evil, and Lucifer. Does this mean the above mentioned will not be present in the tribulation? More to the fact, the word "rapture," is not found in the entire Bible. Note that *harpazo* (caught up) is used to describe the saints gathering to Jesus Christ at the end of the tribulation, not as an early exit before the tribulation.

6. Of our last comment, there are basically four Greek words listed in the Strong's Conc. that describe Jesus Christ's return. With the English equivalents, they are: *parousia* (coming), *anabaino* (come up hither), *harpazo* (caught up), and *sunago* (gather). Of these four, *harpazo* is said to be the rapture word. Although *harpazo* does have the letters "r," "a," and "p," as does the word *parousia,* it hardly constitutes proof a rapture means that Jesus Christ will gather the Church as early as the fifth or sixth trumpets. To suppose so would be to the chagrin of any serious Bible scholar.

The truth is, the word "rapture" cannot be found in the English Bible, or in the original manuscripts. Some claim that Josephus recognized *harpazo* as rapture in Latin, but this is irrelevant because it does not change the timeline when Christ gathers the Church at the seventh trumpet. In other words, it is a timeline matter, not a meaning matter.

More incriminating evidence against a rapture concept is found in the word *ekklesia* (church), which denotes "the called-out ones." It is a group of individuals assembled together as a unifying body in Christ, who is the Head of the Church. Therefore, using simple reasoning, we know that individuals of the body of Christ, no matter how few, represent the Church. With this said, let us research John's Revelation more thoroughly, particularly after Chapter 3, for people who represent the Church. We will call this "individualizing the Church," for, as it is written, where two or three are gathered in Christ's name, every word may be established (Matt. 18:16).

Chapter Five: The Missing Churches After Revelation 3

Here is a limited list of New Testament words and phrases that describe the many membered body of Jesus Christ, all of which are recorded after Revelations 3: Servants, fellow servants, saints, souls of those slain for the Word of God, martyrs, brethren, My People, priests, the righteous, the redeemed, virgins, remnant, first fruits, those of the resurrection, those that "keepeth their garments clean," and have washed their robes, and the called and chosen, etc. To repeat, all of the above are participants, members, believers — whatever you want to call them — are part of the Church, and each are recorded after Revelation 3.

It must be conceded that the Church is well-represented throughout the entire book of John's Revelation. Note also, that in two of three Olivet prophesies taught by Jesus Christ, which address the tribulation period, we find the words "elect" and "election," (Matt. 24:22, 24, 31; Mark 13:20, 22, 27). Should there be any disagreement that the elect and election are part of the Church? Any disagreement must be met with flippancy and disbelief.

Remaining firm on this topic, there is more than ample reason why *ekklesia* is recorded only once after Revelation 3. The outline of John's book is such that, after he dedicated chapters 2 and 3 to introduce and warn the churches of the impending tribulation, there was no urgent reason for him to readdress them as a group until the closing chapter.

It is worthy to note also, that five of seven churches were told to repent. Jesus added that if they did not repent, He would come and remove their candlestick from them. This timeline can only be reconciled as part of the tribulation. It is called the great apostasy, or falling away from Jesus Christ.

A door is also mentioned in Revelation 4:1, and of the two churches that Christ found worthy (Smyrna and Philadelphia), they understand a Jewish fable when they see one. The church of Philadelphia specifically was blessed with an "open door" that no man could shut. This door of truth is Jesus Christ, to whom He tells them, "Him that 'overcometh' will I make a pillar in the temple of God" (Rev. 3:12). But, what do they overcome? They overcome the mark of the beast during the tribulation. Jesus tells them, in no uncertain terms, that He will keep them from the hour of temptation, which means they overcome the Antichrist with knowledge and faith.

In addition, "a voice of a trumpet" initiates a gathering back to Jesus Christ, which pertains to the seventh trumpet (1 Thess. 4:16; 1 Cor. 15:52). A trumpet represents a signal to arms, and it was used to ready the troops for war. It was a warning signal that the enemy is approaching, and the sound resonated throughout the battle. Likewise, the Church is set to do battle against the Antichrist throughout the tribulation. Therefore, God's plan is to use Christians to stand against the enemy in the tribulation. He will cause a certain number of them to speak cloven tongues, which will convince even the dubious gainsayers that Jesus Christ is the Son of God (Titus 1:9).

Now, if the Church has mysteriously vanished before the great battle against the Antichrist ensues, what good is blowing a trumpet, or even having a trumpet? Of course, a trumpet would altogether make sense if the Church was present to do battle against the Antichrist in the tribulation, as it is clearly written. Furthermore, a trumpet was to warn God's people of divine judgment, and the restoration of His people. Apostle John confirms this:

> He that leadeth into captivity shall go into captivity, and he that killeth with the sword must be killed with the sword. Here is the patience and the faith of the saints (Rev. 13:10).

Interpretation: those who believe false doctrine will be led into deception, and those who mislead people with false doctrine will be slain by what they teach. This is what it means to take the mark of beast. But, salvation of the saints involves patience. Those who are willing to stand for truth have the seal of God in their minds, and will not be deceived. Many will be gifted with cloven tongues to spread the gospel, which, as Titus said, will convince even the gainsayers that Jesus Christ is the Son of God.

Part Two

Hiding the Truth

CHAPTER ONE:
2 THESSALONIANS 2:1-12

Now we beseech you, brethren, by the coming of our Lord Jesus Christ, and *by* our gathering together unto him, ² That ye be not soon shaken in mind, or be troubled, neither by spirit, nor by word, nor by letter as from us, as that the day of Christ is at hand. ³ Let no man deceive you by any means: for *that day shall not come*, except there come a falling away first, and that man of sin be revealed, the son of perdition; ⁴ Who opposeth and exalteth himself above all that is called God, or that is worshipped; so that he as God sitteth in the temple of God, showing himself that he is God. ⁵ Remember ye not, that, when I was yet with you, I told you these things? ⁶ Who opposeth and exalteth himself above all that is called God, or that is worshipped; so that he as God sitteth in the temple of God, showing himself that he is God. And now ye know what withholdeth that he might be revealed in his time. ⁷ For the mystery of iniquity doth already work: only he who now letteth *will let*, until he be taken out of the way. ⁸ And then shall that Wicked be revealed, whom the Lord shall consume with the spirit of his mouth, and shall destroy with the brightness of his coming: ⁹ *Even him*, whose coming is after the working of Satan with all power and signs and lying wonders, ¹⁰ And with all deceivableness of unrighteousness in them that perish; because they received not the love of the truth, that they might be saved. ¹¹ And for this cause God shall send them strong delusion, that they should believe a lie: ¹² That they all might be damned who believed not the truth, but had pleasure in unrighteousness. (2 Thess. 2:1-12)

These passages clearly show that Jesus Christ returns to gather the Church *after* the Antichrist's reign on earth. This being true, rapture believers can only respond that part of the Church must be already gone at this point. But, where is this written? And, who is this "part" of the Church? Is the Church taken from earth in parts?

Paul's introduction is the key to his message. The subject is the coming of the Lord, and he warns fellow Christians (his brethren) that Jesus Christ does not return to earth until *after* the falling away takes place, and the Antichrist is revealed. This means that the Church will witness the working of Satan, with all power and signs and lying wonders, before Jesus returns to gather them in His Spirit. It is their destiny.

Let there be no misunderstanding to Paul's words. He clearly states that believers should watch for a sinful man, also called the son of perdition (son of death), to be revealed before Jesus Christ returns to earth. This is a clear directive from the apostle. The Antichrist will be a powerful leader "who opposeth and exalteth himself above all that is called God, or that is worshipped; so that he as God sitteth in the temple of God, showing himself that he is God." He will come working with all power, signs, and lying wonders, and with all deceivableness of unrighteousness in them who perish before Jesus Christ returns in His glory (see Isa. 14:13-15). These things Judas did not do, nor will he return to earth and claim to be God.

It is blasphemous and a foolish notion indeed to apply Satan's wicked attributes to a weak man like Judas of Iscariot. It is certain, and beyond all doubt, that the "man of sin," and the "son of perdition" are epithets of one entity: Satan, the Antichrist. This is confirmed by his actions:

> Who opposeth and exalteth himself above all that is called God, or that is worshipped; so that he as God sitteth in the temple of God, showing himself that he is God. [4]

Even more, the great prophet, Habakkuk, depicts Satan as a proud "man," that is as death (Hab. 2:5). "Proud man" is the Hebrew *yahiyr geber*, which means "a supernatural man." Habakkuk was writing about the coming judgment that would fall upon the wicked in the last generation, which could only describe Satan as the Antichrist. Speaking of the word "man," representing a supernatural entity, the mighty angel Gabriel means "*man* of God."

The false doctrine that identifies Judas Iscariot as the man of sin and the son of perdition must be rejected as unsound and deceptive. This is due to the mere fact that Judas did not, and will not in the future, exalt himself above all that is called God, which proves the point. Judas also did not want to be worshipped, so that as God, he sits in the temple of God, showing that he is God. This confirms that he is not part of Paul's prophecy. In fact, Judas, after repenting for betrayed innocent blood, cast his most prized possession of silver to the chief priests and elders in the temple to show his great remorse of betrayal. As the saying goes, actions speak louder than words.

The truth is, Paul, being a scholar of the manuscripts, was citing Isaiah, who said Lucifer (Satan) is the one who will claim to be God in the near future, not Judas (quotation marks mine):

> How art thou fallen from heaven, O "Lucifer, son of the morning!" how art thou cut down to the ground, "which

> didst weaken the nations!" [13] For thou hast said in thine heart, "I will ascend into heaven, I will exalt my throne above the stars of God: I will sit also upon the mount of the congregation, in the sides of the north: [14] I will ascend above the heights of the clouds; I will be like the most High" (14:10-14).

Any rational person who is not indoctrinated too deeply into the traditions of men can surely understand that the great apostasy or falling away from Jesus Christ happens immediately before the seventh trump, at which time, Jesus Christ returns to earth to gather the saints, and reign as King of kings and Lord of lords.

So, therefore, we may ask, what causes the falling away? Paul tells us. It is Satan's appearance who will oppose and exalt himself above all that is called God. "All that is called God," means that Satan will claim to be the God of *all* the religions on earth, for world religions collectively have their own concept and ideology of who or what is God.

It is sad but true, that the world at large will accept a false messiah when he comes at the sixth trump claiming to be God. By Daniel's own words, he will come in peaceably, prosperously, wonderfully, and destroy with flatteries (Dan. 8:24, 25; 11:21, 24). He will give the world the illusion that He is God, the Savior of the world. Paul called this great deception the *apostasy*, or in English, the falling away (2 Thess. 2:3). This is when a person leaves a particular belief for another belief in a moment of great deception.

This is why, according to the Strong's Conc., "antichrist" means "instead of Christ;" he comes instead of Christ. When we refer back to the first seal, we find that Jesus warned His listeners that there would be many who come in His name, claiming to be sent by God, but they would preach a false Antichrist doctrine. "Let no *man* deceive you," especially pertains to the

Antichrist, as he is the "*man* of sin" that Paul identifies in his second letter to the Thessalonians. Paul adds that to deny the Antichrist, is to reject the mark of the beast. This involves being sealed with the knowledge that Jesus returns after the man of sin is revealed, the son of perdition, the only son of death.

In simple terms, accepting the mark means that you will accept the Antichrist as Jesus Christ, and wed out of season, instead of waiting for the true Christ to return. This is why Jesus said: "Woe unto those who are with child, and to them that give suck in those days." A majority of the world will hasten to marry "instead of Christ," and impregnate themselves with deception, while others will wait to marry "the anointed Christ," at the marriage supper of the Lamb.

Now, it has been suggested that, "only he who letteth will let, till *he be taken out of the way*" (verse 7), means that the Holy Spirit is taken out of the way. However, this is categorically and immensely incorrect. For the word "letteth" is a transitive verb, which means that it must transfer to (or be associated with) the aforesaid subject, that which is the Antichrist (the man of sin and the son of perdition — *verses 3-6*) who comes to deceive the world. Therefore, it cannot mean that the Holy Spirit is taken out of the way.

Nowhere in the Bible does it say that the Holy Spirit is taken to heaven, much less that it is removed from earth, adding the obvious point that the Holy Spirit is ubiquitous, for God exists in things in heaven and earth. It is far beyond a stretch to say that a single man's vision, whether he was on earth physically, or taken to heaven spiritually, represents a rapture of the Church. To make such a claim is not consistent with quality scholarship. Moreover, how can a non-Christian become a saint, with no Holy Spirit present to convert them? The Bible makes it clear that the sealing of the 144,000 Israelites (Rev. 7:1-8), which obliges the Holy Spirit, takes place during the tribulation.

Equipped with this knowledge, we are now prepared to understand the sealing of the remnant-Israelites that God will utilize in the tribulation. The sealing of God's people includes the gift of the cloven tongues to a select number of Christians. It is the Power from upon High that ensures success to the calling out of thousands upon thousands from every nation and creed to serve the Living God. As it is written, a multitude too great to number from every creed, kindred, and tongue will come out of the great tribulation, having washed their robes in the blood of the Lamb (Rev. 7:9).

Many pastors call these saints "tribulation saints," which is an unbiblical term like the word "rapture." Instead of using the biblical word "saints," or even "Christians," a diverse term is used, as though they are somewhat inferior to the first group taken. Moreover, because rapture preachers teach that all Christians are "taken" before the tribulation, they have no other recourse but to label the "soon-to-be-Christians" something else.

May I propose that the opposite may be true? Recalling Matthew 25:1-13, of the five foolish virgins that fell short, i.e., foolish Christians who are deceived in the tribulation, perhaps God must remove the foolish and unprepared Christians, to make way for the prepared and wiser Christians to face the trials of the tribulation, as so required of a tested believer.

Whatever the case may be, the Bible calls them saints, not tribulation saints. In truth, a saint pre-trib is a saint mid-trib, and is a saint post-trib. Their destiny was preordained before the foundations of the world to engage in a spiritual battle against the Antichrist. God chooses only the best-prepared to do His work. Sadly, rapture believers believe that the best prepared are taken from earth at the most pivotal battle against the Antichrist.

Nonetheless, with the Greek making everything so clear, this has caused some dissension within the ranks of rapture teachers. For, some now advance the opinion, as a backup plan, to allow for two interpretations, that the phrase "he be taken out of the way," is the Church taken out of the way.

How convenient, except for the very important fact that the Church is the bride of Christ, which is feminine. As clearly as Paul put forth the truth of the matter, many preachers remain firm to their convictions that "he" is the Church. So, as it is with human pride, admitting a wrong can be problematic. If one can accept the male pronoun "he," (instead of the female pronoun "she,") as the Church, the bride of Christ, then by all means enjoy resolution.

Chapter Two: Grace Means Tribulation for Christians

The above statement was echoed through the pews of a church by a well-known pastor. He made this statement to pacify those who were fearful about going through the tribulation. He went on to explain that Christians are victorious in the age of grace; therefore, they do not have to go through the tribulation. Ironically, another renowned pastor said something similar, that God would spare Christians from facing the Antichrist, because there is no condemnation to those who are in Christ Jesus.

However, it must be understood that many Christians in the age of grace faced brutal consequences for their faith in Christ. They were condemned, beaten, tortured, beheaded, and slain for following the teachings of Jesus Christ. In fact, Paul was told by Ananias that God would show him great things that he must suffer for Jesus Christ (Acts 9:16).

Acknowledging the fact that early church Christians suffered greatly for spreading the gospel, why would Christians today be exempt from spreading the gospel in the tribulation? In fact, when speaking of the end times, Jesus identified martyrdom as the fifth seal. Apostle John wrote that Christians would face troubling times in the tribulation, and that they should be willing to give their lives for Jesus Christ (Matt. 6:25; 10:39; John 12:25; Rev. 2:7; 3:2,5). Paul said that we are killed all day long, and we are accounted as sheep for the slaughter (Rom. 8:36).

So, what did these two preachers mean when they said that Christians will bypass the tribulation because of God's grace, and that there is no condemnation to those who are in Jesus Christ? Well, in short, they were trying to pacify rather than rectify.

Let us begin by connecting verse two to complete Paul's thought:

> There is therefore now no condemnation to them which are in Christ Jesus, who walk not after the flesh, but after the Spirit. ² For the law of the Spirit of life in Christ Jesus hath made me free from the law of sin and death.

The subject here, Paul explains, is the law of Christ and the law of sin. Paul makes the point that Christians cannot be condemned to hellfire on judgment day, for Heaven is their salvation. This is not to say that they cannot be condemned in other ways, but eternal damnation is not possible for a believer.

Simply put, "no condemnation" pertains to final judgment. It has nothing to do with a Christian's daily walk in Christ. Jesus came to teach us, not to condemn us. He told the woman at the well who had five husbands, going on six, "I do not condemn thee, but go and sin no more" (John 8:11). Let us not, therefore, confuse condemnation with commission. To be a witness in the tribulation is a commission, not condemnation. The former pertains to every day; the latter pertains to judgment day.

Chapter Three: Cloven Tongues

The words "cloven tongues" are found only once in the Bible. The key word, cloven (Greek, *diamerizo*) means "disunite, or to differ." Put together with "tongues" (language), it means an unnatural language or heavenly language. This is entirely distinct from a natural or earthly language, such as Spanish, German, or Chinese. *Diamerizo* is used in Acts 2:3, on the Day of Pentecost, and is commonly referred to as the "Pentecostal Tongue." It was poured out by the Holy Spirit to every nation under Heaven that attended the great feast, all of whom understood it in their own language — even in their own dialect! Plainly put, it was a heavenly miracle. Therefore, it may be said that cloven tongues are a miracle wonder poured out by the Holy Spirit, that which is not earthly and is extremely rare.

Now, by comparing *diamerizo*, the Pentecostal cloven tongues, to Apostle Paul's discourse on speaking in tongues (speaking earthly languages), we find a substantial difference between them. Paul's unknown tongue is a common language, or equally said, an earthly language that which is not rare. More directly, it implies a person that learns a foreign language – like an English person learning Spanish, German, or Chinese. This is why Paul instructed those who prophesy in an unknown tongue (foreign language), to have an interpreter present to express proper thought and meaning; otherwise, as Paul said, they are speaking into the air (1 Cor. 14:9). It would do no good to speak English to a group of Hispanics or Chinese if neither understood the English language.

Thus considered, we see that Paul's "tongues" is an earthly thing; whereas, "cloven tongues" is a heavenly thing. Misunderstanding this tenant has led to much confusion to the speaking in tongues topic. It is therefore essential, if we are to maintain proper understanding of the cloven tongue's topic, to distinguish it from speaking in an earthly language; which, when a person can speak multiple languages, is commonly known as bilingual.

The crux of our discussion is to clarify that Paul's tongue discourse to the Corinthians has nothing to do with the cloven tongues miracle on Pentecost Day recorded by Luke. It should also be well-noted that there is the element of dual prophecy connected with cloven tongues, for it will be gifted to a chosen few in the tribulation.

Hence, the speaking in cloven tongues debate is not so much if it is true, but when will it take place, and what is its purpose? To answer these questions suitably, it requires a brief review of the rapture theory.

Chapter Four: The Rapture Theory

Although the rapture theory is founded on a hoard of biblical misinterpretations, it has literally deceived millions of people — primarily Christians — the ones who should know better. Yet, the truth is that it can be easily discounted by using the very Word men misuse to espouse it.

Christians are warned throughout the Bible to prepare themselves for this great event; yet, only a few are listening. However, after the sealing of the one hundred and forty-four thousand Israelites (not Jews), many more will listen. Nevertheless, the point is why would a Christian wait until the tribulation to understand the truth about this evil doctrine when they could be preparing themselves, as God's spiritual frontrunners, to defeat Satan's evil coup in the tribulation?

This is why the cloven tongues debate is so important. It is every Christian's calling to be spiritually adept with full knowledge of who the Antichrist is, and to know the times and seasons of the end days. A select number of believers will be blessed with cloven tongues to spread the gospel around the world, which will call many people of all creeds, nations, and tongues to Jesus Christ.

Being on the wrong side of right on the rapture argument endangers one to be wholly unequipped spiritually, mentally, and physically to face the Antichrist when he arrives on the world scene. In fact, to add a tit-for-tat argument to our discussion, there is a popular saying among Christians that gives them every reason to believe in God. The saying is: "It is far better to believe that there is a God and find out that there isn't, then not to believe in God and find out that there is." To this simple, yet profound saying, we must all agree then that "it is far better to believe that there is not a rapture and find out that there is, then to believe there is a rapture and find out that there isn't." Not a single Christian should argue against this sound reasoning, for they themselves understand the rationale behind it.

To conceive the rapture concept as to how Christians gather back to Christ, we must accept, or try to imagine, the thought that at a particular moment, in a twinkling of an eye, "the dead in Christ," which is to say, buried corpses — rise in mid-air to meet the Lord in the clouds; then, at some time later, a second group of Christians are "caught up together with them," to meet the Lord. As one preacher I heard say from his pulpit: "Do not be around a graveyard during the rapture."

Now the immediate question arises: how can one body of believers rise first, ahead of a second group (or *before* a second group), and still rise "together" to meet the Lord in the air? Does the second group rise faster, so as to catch-up to the first group before they meet Christ somewhere in the air together? Or does it mean that two separate groups are not really separate once they are in the air? Or are they separate technically, but not spiritually? We are not sure what they mean.

No matter, for they also believe that there is yet a third group that is gathered to Christ later at the seventh trump. This third group, evidently, is not taken together with the other two groups that are taken before the sixth trump. We say before the sixth trump because the Antichrist comes at the sixth trump, which is after the rapture. So, in essence, they believe that there is a rapture as early as the fifth trump, of which nothing could be more unbiblical.

When we compare this rather difficult-to-follow rapture concept — which has three gatherings to Christ at three separate intervals and is contrary to a natural one-time harvest — with a second-chance doctrine to a non-rapture viewpoint, which is one body of Christians gathered together at one time and no second chance doctrine (Rev. 14:14-16), we see clarity in the latter, and confusion with the prior. This is because God is not the author of confusion, but the God of peace and understanding.

The Bible makes it clear that during the tribulation, a great multitude, which no man could number, of all nations, kindreds, people, and tongues, will wash their robes in the blood of the Lamb. This number depicts billions of people that would supposedly miss a pre-trib rapture, yet would be saved in the tribulation. This contradicts a one-chance doctrine that is taught in most churches.

But, the question is not so much if Christians will be gathered unto Jesus Christ, because they will, it is more a question of *when* they will be gathered? It will happen at the seventh trump after the tribulation.

For the distinct purpose of painting a picture for the minds-eye to behold billions of Christians worldwide vanishing into thin air, presented forward is an extensive supposition on this very topic. It is written, on the part of caution, for those who would rest their soul in a rapture concept before seriously analyzing all the implications involved in such an earth-blown catastrophe.

Interestingly, before we delve into this topic, a vivid depiction of the massive carnage a rapture would create is rarely spoken at the pulpits. Who can blame those uneasy about teaching something so horrific that perhaps it would change the minds of those being taught that a rapture makes no sense. Hollywood, on the other hand, has profited much from an array of movies that have entertained the public with rather "unrealistic" and "nonbiblical" satires of the rapture. (Are they poking fun at foolish Christians?) When there is money for the taking, Hollywood is always most obliging.

Yet, this suppression from the pulpits, especially by those caught up in it, and profit the most from it, can only be explained by the mere fact that it is wholly unrealistic. Although God uses supernatural events to fulfill His will, a disappearing act of several billion people from earth, and the horrific carnage of innocent people left in its wake, is not one of them. With this said, let us imagine, or try to imagine, with utmost realism, the devastation involved with a premature rapture of the Church.

To set our minds in motion to the realism of such a nonbiblical event, we will begin with a countless number of social implications. According to world population in 2020 (http://esa.un.org/unpd/wpp/unpp/p2k0data.asp), children under the age of fifteen – perhaps under the age of spiritual accountability – make up twenty-six percent of close to eight billion people on earth. This is close to an amazing two billion children that would be raptured by a loving and fair God. Jesus said, "Unless you come to me as little children ye shall not enter the kingdom of heaven" (Matt. 18:3-5; 19:14).

Of those who would consider Jesus's words evidence of a rapture; that is, that it would be incredulous to the highest degree to sentence young children, particularly babes and suckling, to such devastation in the tribulation, let it be firmly noted that, as it is written in Daniel 11:21-24, the Antichrist will obtain the kingdom (convert the world) by acts of kindness, fabricated love, peace, prosperity, and flatteries. His goal is to win souls, not to lose souls, and this cannot be accomplished by torturing children — including their parents.

Now, the thought of two billion children raptured from their parents or other substitute caretakers, is inconceivable and difficult to imagine such a high-level of trauma. It would be an unspeakable nightmare, which would comprise more than two billion people; incalculable suicides would add even more deaths to the falling numbers of people missing from earth. To be blunt, the panic-stricken world could not recuperate from such a devastating event. In addition to the number of suicides, millions more would perish from the surfeit of accidents created from a rapture.

How many innocent people would be involved in car accidents, and other modes of travel, including air, water, rail, etc.? It is also certain that moments after a worldwide-rapture-catastrophe, shortage in every category of petroleum products, primarily gas and oil, would be rationed or altogether halted. With no gas to run vehicles, transportation would not be an option. How many people dependent on medicines, and other medical treatments, would needlessly suffer and eventually die? This would not only involve more natural deaths, but it would involve more suicides by family members and friends distressed over the overwhelming horror.

Numerous others would suffer heart attacks and strokes from such trauma. Countless others would die from many other vile occurrences here not mentioned, but the major points have been made to suffice an unrealistic acceptance of the rapture concept.

Yet, what has been presented thus far is the tip of the iceberg, for many other things must be considered when speaking of such a cataclysmic event. The immense crimes of pillaging would undoubtedly cause many more deaths around the world. Those incarcerated would be set free, or escape, causing more deaths and chaos. It is equally certain that, in the spirit of desperation, even good people would do horrendous and criminal things to survive the horrors. Schools of every sort, including universities, colleges, vocational and trade institutions, other faculties of higher education, etc., would cease to exist. Banks would collapse. Manufacturing and industries of every kind would shut down.

Real estate businesses would cease to exist, along with a myriad of other commerce. Stock markets worldwide would collapse. Governments would gridlock. Electrical grids would shut down. Sports, and the millions it employed, would also be adversely affected. At this juncture, it is safe to say that we have added at least a half billion more people that would perish within weeks after a rapture. This puts the total missing people from earth at about two and a half billion.

As shown, to this point the world's population would be approximately four and a half billion people, or perhaps much less. But there are numerous others who would also be omitted from the tribulation. According to religious demographics, approximately thirty-one percent of the world's population are professing Christians (http://en.m.wikipedia.org). Of this percentage, the number of children under fifteen is unknown; however, it is certain not to include infants and newborns. If we consent to half of the thirty-three percent being so-called ready for the rapture, then close to one billion adult Christians would be raptured. However, according to the common church expression "once saved, always saved," to balance out the children under fifteen that may be included in the thirty-three percent, perhaps this number would be closer to two billion people. This leaves approximately two to three billion people remaining on earth to go through the tribulation.

Notwithstanding, we have not yet considered other sectors of the population that would be spared from God's judgement in the tribulation, starting with the countless handicapped with mental disorders, the chronically sick, the underprivileged, those with mental illnesses, including many other disadvantaged people. According to demographics, fifteen percent of the world's population, or one billion, have mental illnesses of some kind (http://ourworldindata.org/mental-health).

In addition, there are those who have never heard the gospel, or have been taught improperly, that are in all likelihood not held accountable. This number of people is certainly difficult to pinpoint, but it is a factor to be considered. Whether or not this group of people would be raptured, or protected by God in some way, is debatable; perhaps it is a good question for rapture believers to answer.

There are countless other things to scrutinize with a rapture concept. We have not yet mentioned that there would not be enough doctors, nurses, nurse aids, social workers, medical aids, hospital administrators, and supervisors, etc., to aid in the overwhelming sickness and diseases that would result from a rapture. This would cause such an enormity of deaths, that it is hard to fathom how many. Miscarriages and deaths from pregnancy would doubtless be an overwhelming number. In Matthew 24:19 (including other Olivet prophecies), Jesus warned of those who are with child, and give suck (nursing) in those days (tribulation days). So, how can a woman breastfeed an infant who is not there?

The truth to the above reference is that Jesus was not speaking literally; He was speaking spiritually. He did not say "women that give suck," He said "them" that give suck. "Them" is a spiritual reference to people, no gender intended, who are impregnated with Satan's flood of lies during the tribulation (Dan. 11:22; Matt. 7:25-27; 24:39; Luke 6:48, 17:27; Rev. 12:15, 16). Birthing a child has always been a blessing from upon High, and that fact will never change. God will not take the miracle of childbirth, and change it into a curse.

To this point, it is safe to say that less than a billion people will remain to survive the tribulation. The questions never cease when realism is attached to our rapture topic. For example, how would the remaining population bury the manifold death count? Who would excavate all the graves, and where would they bury them? Who would officiate the untold millions of funerals, and what would they say? There is reference to the burying of the dead from the battle of Hamon-gog that takes seven months to complete (Ezek. 39:11-14); however, this battle is post-trib, not pre-trib, and neither is it to be taken literally, for immediately after, Jesus returns to destroy the wicked. At His Second Advent, He ushers in the millennial age, where people inherit incorruptible bodies as the flesh is destroyed.

The term "burying the dead" is a spiritual reference to people who are spiritually dead (deceived); and, if you look around the world today, you see spiritually-dead people everywhere. The rapture theory has certainly contributed to it. Now, to be quite candid about our next segment, it is unconceivable to imagine the social implications of even 100,000 people vanishing from earth, much less several billion. The world would be disrupted in such a dramatic fashion that life itself, as it had existed for thousands of years, would cease to be even minutely close to its original state — if it would be possible to exist even a year longer. This alone conflicts with God's promise that the earth will continue as created forever (Gen. 8:22; Eccl. 1:4). Yet, the bogus rapture plot would change the earth as we know it, and would alter, if not utterly stop, the way doctrine is taught both spiritually and secularly. This includes the way we function on a daily basis.

Yet, the Bible says that a great multitude, which no man could number, will be saved. We are asked to believe that the Antichrist will reconcile the world's troubles with peace and prosperity. Supposing that the Antichrist had this power, would he not then be a god to believe in, or a heavenly entity as powerful as God? So, how are Christians able to identify the real God?

To shift our attention politically, it is clear that God intended our world to have a designated working class of people in all walks of life. Some are richer than others, and some are more powerful, but together, all sustain the world economies. So, what happens to this global system when four to six billion people disappear (some in a twinkling of an eye, and others more gradually, by death)? For that matter, what if one billion people disappeared? The fact is, there would not be enough people to sustain a one-world system, and what would the Antichrist do with this dilemma?

Furthermore, there would not be enough farmers to plant, and consequently, to harvest the land, and feed the people. Only Jesus could feed so many with so little, but He is not scheduled to be here until the seventh trump, and the Antichrist is not a farmer. It is true that he is granted sufficient power to deceive the nations, but he does not possess divine power — he can only attempt to mimic God's power. Although he will perform miracles and bring fire from Heaven, he cannot outdo, or equally perform, Jesus Christ's miracles.

Besides, as mentioned, the Bible says that seedtime and harvest shall never cease (Gen. 8:22). In other words, the agriculture industry will continue to sustain itself, with no interruptions. Put plainly, that means we have no right or reason to believe that such a catastrophic force as a rapture will actually occur on earth. It is self-evident that no man, whether possessed by Satan or not, could deceive the world into believing that he is God after such a mind-blowing event. No miracles, magic wand, or pixie dust, could sooth the hearts of men after such a travesty.

The thought of several billion people instantly disappearing from the earth would destroy the whole human race — even many less would have the same result. In truth, a rapture of billions of people stands in opposition to God's overall plan for mankind, and His creation. We are asked to believe throughout all this unimaginable carnage, that a mere flesh man is going to stand in a temple in Jerusalem and claim to be God? To believe this, one would be accounted as the many sheep for the slaughter.

Just imagine, with most Christians living in the western hemisphere, which includes up to seventy-five percent of all Christians, and such a large portion of them vanishing from North America, how long would it take for those remaining in the eastern hemisphere to occupy the land of the free? How long would it take them to clean up the enormous carnage, if they are willing to do so? Does the Antichrist possess sufficient power to snap his finger to heal such a worldwide travesty? The answer is categorically "no."

Please observe the following: Using a world population of about eight billion people (2022 consensus). here is the estimated world population after a rapture:

People raptured:

1. Children under fifteen: two billion.
2. Born-again Christians: two billion.
3. Underprivileged (spiritually innocent): half a billion
Sub-total: four-and-a-half billion.

Deaths from a rapture:

1. Suicides: millions
2. Accidents (travel, explosions, collapsed structures of all kinds, etc.,): several millions.
3. Medical casualties and sickness: several millions.
4. Pillaging, murder, etc.: tens of thousands.
5. Other travesties not included: thousands of thousands.

Total: five billion.

Total world population remaining: three billion.

As astounding as this woeful picture of a rapture is, there are yet more serious implications to consider, beginning with religion. Of the unprepared Christians, those who were not ready for the rapture, or who may be called carnal-Christians, which according to demographics, is approximately one-and-a half billion Christians (about half of thirty-three percent of eight billion), it can be sure that most, if not all, would find solace to repent to the true God — even from their knees (Isa. 45:23; Rom. 14:11). This act of humility would not save them from the tribulation; however, it would greatly influence their decision to readily accept the hardships of a tribulation, and become a saint (Rev. 7:9-14). Speak of an incentive for choosing salvation over death the alternative. This torrid experience would surely accomplish that goal. It would be the proverbial: first time, shame on the world; second time, shame on me. To ignore God twice, especially while experiencing Bible prophecy first hand, would be unimaginable.

Now, it is very apparent and quite biblical that not only would innocent people repent from their evil deeds, but a rapture of so many people would convert even the most stoic secularist, infidel, or atheist. There is reference to some of the more wicked that will not repent from their evil deeds (Rev. 16:11), but this is before the seventh trump when it is written that "all" will succumb to the Living God.

Continuing forward with the math dilemma of a rapture, the Bible makes it clear that all Israel shall be saved (Rom. 11:26). Thus, we can consent to the fact that an innumerable number of physical Israelites will be saved in the tribulation (others will require the millennium age). Hence, with billions of people already missing from a rapture, including so many untimely deaths, and perhaps also to include a higher number of Israelites redeemed by the blood of Christ, how do we reconcile the placement of billions of non-Christians on earth? As one can plainly see, the possibility of a rapture is not only illogical, it is both spiritually and mathematically impossible.

It is well worth noting that higher awareness to predicting the "any moment" theory began to heat up mid-twentieth century. Yet, no rapture has yet to occur — though millions of people did fall prey to the Y2K debacle at the turn of the century. Countless people still run scared every time a sundog, or other brilliant objects, appear in the sky. Thousands of children have experienced great trauma by assuming that they have been "left behind," when on occasion, they return to an unexpected, empty home. This is an outright shame, of which this author has experienced.

Nevertheless, the truth is, there was no rapture as predicted in the 1950s, or the 60s, 70s, 80s, 90s, or even up to the year 2022. This is because there is not going to be a rapture prior to Christ's Second Coming, which is post-trib. The Great prophet, Jeremiah, had strong comments about those who falsify Bible doctrine with predictions of peace when there is no peace prior to the will of the Living God. (Of these times and seasons read: Jer. 8:7-15; 42:11-19.)

Probably the most incredulous element to the fifth or sixth trumpet rapture lie, lies in population statistics. Again, using conservative figures who will be here and who will not be here during the tribulation, we find that only a billion, or two billion max, would remain to witness the full tribulation period — which is believed to be three and a half years. This diminutive number of people could not rightly sustain a world economy even for a day. At this juncture, it must also be realized that there are countless other factors unnoticed, due to this unimaginable topic. This adds even more deaths to an already ridiculous number.

Attempting to rap our heads around a "rapture-vision," let us also consider the effect that the resurrection of Jesus Christ (a single man) had on the world to billions of people resurrecting into thin air. During the hardened times of the early Christian era many Judeans did not believe that Jesus was God because they could not imagine God having a corporal existence. Although a certain mass of people, both great and small, witnessed the crucifixion and burial only five hundred plus witnessed His resurrection (1 Cor. 15:5-8).

Many rumors circulated that Jesus' body was either stolen or removed from the sepulcher, which suppressed, at least to some degree, the astonishing effect of the resurrection. Yet, the enormous effect it had on the human race is nothing short of a miraculous wonderment. However, with today's advancement in communications, it may be argued that the disappearing act of even one person from earth would have more impact than the resurrection of Jesus Christ — not in space of time, of course, but in the realm of the human psyche. Truly, the effect on the human race would be staggering.

Chapter Four: The Rapture Theory

Realistically, if a thousand people witnessed a YouTube video presentation showing a single person disappearing before the camera's eye, the world would be turned upside down. Now, imagine four or five billion vanishing. It is probable that all people, perhaps the Antichrist himself, would faint or go into spiritual cardiac arrest. Consider, if you will, the mind-boggling effects the UFO phenomenon has had on the world alone. Rapture supporters perhaps should consider the fact that Jesus did not mention a pre-trib rapture of the Church in His Olivet prophecies — and if there was an early rapture of the Church to be mentioned, this is where He would have announced it (Matt. 24; Mark 13; Luke 21).

In these passages, the disciples asked a specific question: when shall these things be, and what shall be the "sign of thy coming," and "the end of the world?" The disciples could not have asked clearer and pointed questions. No rational person could possibly believe that such a cataclysmic world event — or perhaps we should say, such a universal, cosmical, extraterrestrial, astronomical event of such enormous proportions, where billions of people vanish event — would not have been revealed by Jesus Christ. To deny this is the true definition of blinded Israel.

Of the pastors who realize that Jesus did not teach an early rapture of the Church in any sermons or parable, including the most prominent Olivet Prophesies, yet still hold to the rapture concept, they excuse Jesus's forgetfulness to the assumption that the Church must be already gone at this point. In fact, they actually leverage it as a point of proof for a rapture doctrine. The extreme problem with this failing, and so-called logic, is that it would not matter if the Church was gone, for such an extraordinary event brought upon the world would certainly be taught to inform all men that they need a Savior; after all, this is the great commission.

Finally, in sum of our long rapture discourse, to believe that Jesus Christ would fail to mention a rapture could be compared to Moses describing how God delivered the Israelites from the Egyptians, without mentioning how the Red Sea was divided. Or, how the Israelites defeated Jericho without mentioning how the great walls crumbled to the ground. Or, how David killed Goliath without mentioning a sling and five stones. The obvious conclusion in which we must agree is that Jesus did not mention an early rapture of the Church because there is no early rapture of the Church.

Quite plainly put, and for the very purpose of this book, the only gathering that Jesus Christ taught, which every believer must adhere to, happens after the tribulation at the seventh trumpet (Matt. 24: 29-31; Mark 13:24-27; Luke 21:27-28).

www.ingramcontent.com/pod-product-compliance
Ingram Content Group UK Ltd.
Pitfield, Milton Keynes, MK11 3LW, UK
UKHW041956230426
12048UKWH00008B/363